Tudors (1485–1603)

| 0 | 1000 AD | 2000 AD |

–146BC)

Anglo-Saxons (450–1066)

Victorians (1837–1901)

Romans (700BC–476AD)

Vikings (800–1066/1400)

Contents

Look up the **bold** words in the glossary
on page 32 of this book.

enry VIII dies. His son,
Edward VI, is king

Henry VIII's other daughter
becomes Queen Elizabeth I

Sir Francis Drake begins his
circumnavigation of the world

The first permanent
colony in America

| 1555 | 1565 | 1575 | 1585 | 1595 | 1605 |

ary, Edward's elder sister,
Catholic, becomes Mary I

The playwright, William
Shakespeare, is born

Mary, Queen of
Scots, is executed

The Spanish
Armada

Elizabeth I dies

Meet the Tudors

This is the red and white Tudor rose.

The **Tudors** were kings and queens of England who reigned between 1485 and 1603, that is between five and four hundred years ago. They were all descended from Henry Tudor, who became King Henry VII (Henry the seventh).

Henry VII's second son, Henry, became Henry VIII of England. Henry VII's daughter, Mary, was married to the King of France. Another daughter, Margaret, was married to the king of Scotland. In this way, later on the kings and queens of France and Scotland could claim the English throne. This led to trouble all through Tudor times.

Henry VIII wanted to divorce his first wife. However, the Roman Catholic church would not let him. To get around this problem, Henry founded the Church of England.

Henry VIII had six wives: Catherine of Aragon (divorced), Anne Boleyn (beheaded), Jane Seymour (died), Anne of Cleves (divorced), Kathryn Howard (beheaded) and Katherine Parr (who outlived Henry).

Queen Elizabeth I, also called 'Good Queen Bess". She never married, so she was the last of the Tudors.

Did you know... ?

- The Tudor rose is made using the red rose, a symbol of Lancaster, and the white rose, a symbol of York. The Tudors' idea was to unite these powerful peoples and so stop **civil war**.
- Nearly all of the Tudor kings and queens had an important part in Britain's history. Henry VII was followed by Henry VIII, then by his three children – Edward VI (who died young), Mary I and lastly Elizabeth I (who all died childless).

Q Why were Henry VIII and Elizabeth I called Tudors?

New church, new wealth

In Tudor times England broke away from the Roman Catholic church. It happened like this.

Henry VIII was a dashing young prince who was popular with the ladies. But as a king he needed sons to rule England after him.

Henry was married to Catherine of Aragon. She bore him a son, who soon died. Then she gave birth to Mary. By now Catherine was too old to have any more children, so Henry needed a new wife.

The Roman Catholic church refused to give Henry a divorce, so he set up the Church of England with himself as head, then gave himself the divorce he needed.

On the way out: The Roman Catholic church, the pope, cardinals, monks, abbots, abbeys and monasteries. Many monateries were destroyed in Tudor times. This is why they are ruins today.

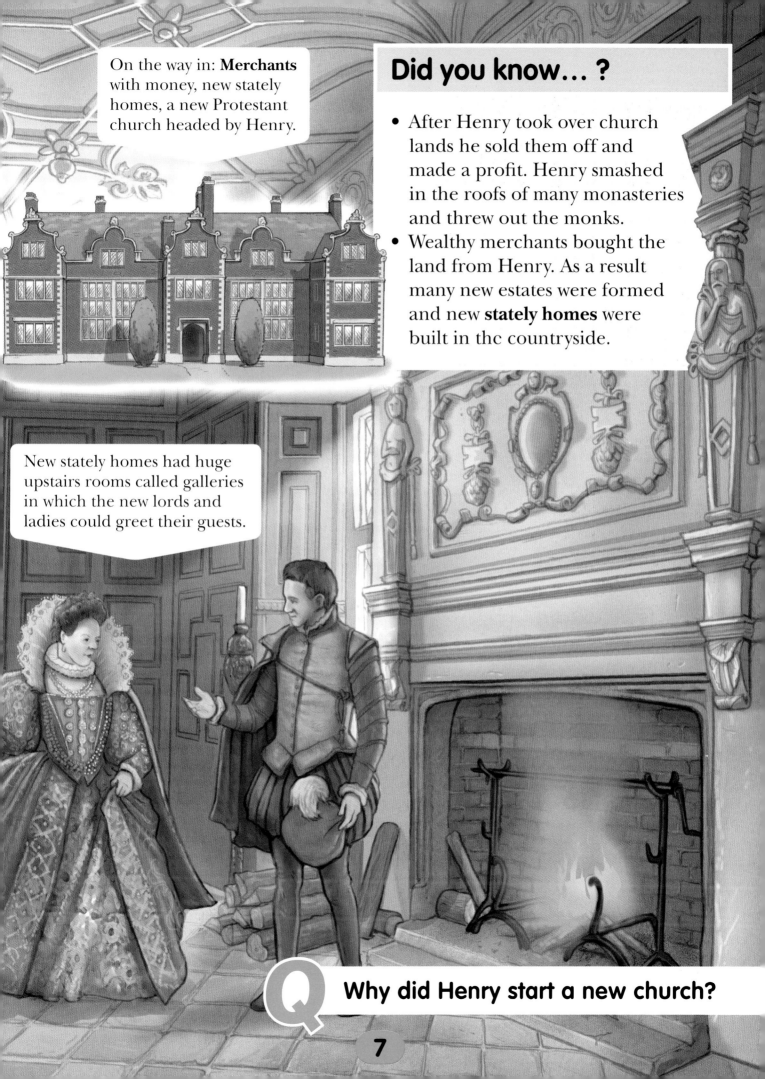

On the way in: **Merchants** with money, new stately homes, a new Protestant church headed by Henry.

Did you know… ?

- After Henry took over church lands he sold them off and made a profit. Henry smashed in the roofs of many monasteries and threw out the monks.
- Wealthy merchants bought the land from Henry. As a result many new estates were formed and new **stately homes** were built in the countryside.

New stately homes had huge upstairs rooms called galleries in which the new lords and ladies could greet their guests.

Why did Henry start a new church?

Rich and poor

In Tudor times there were a small number of wealthy people and a large number of poor people.

It was very clear whether you were wealthy or poor by the way you dressed.

A wealthy lord and lady in front of their large home.

If you were wealthy you wore very fancy clothes you couldn't possibly work in.

If you were poor, you wore clothes that were hard wearing and simple to make, and that could easily be mended.

Poor people in front of their rented cottage.

Q Why did rich and poor wear different clothes?

What rich and poor ate

There was plenty of food during Tudor times – if you could afford it.

The wealthy had a wide variety of foods. They were made more tasty by using **spices** from overseas. Meals would contain many different servings.

The poor sat down to eat a single serving of very simple food. How much they got depended on the harvest. If the harvest had been poor they might have to add ground-up acorns to the flour to see them through the year.

Poor people sat down on benches to eat at rough tables. They ate from wooden plates and used only a knife and spoon.

Did you know… ?

- Dinner in a rich person's home might consist of over seven courses.
- If you were rich, you could expect many kinds of roasted meat and wine on your table.
- If you were poor you would be eating ryebread, pottage (stew), fish if you were lucky, and you would be drinking beer (yes, even if you were a child, because the water was not safe to drink).
- A pomander was a sweet-smelling object made from food but not to be eaten. It could be worn on a belt or carried. It was quite helpful in the days when no one washed and there was foul-smelling rubbish everywhere.

Rich people ate off a table that might be covered with a cloth. They would eat from metal (pewter) plates and would use glasses for their wine.

Q **What was the difference between rich people's and poor people's food?**

A Tudor village

When Tudor times began in 1485 just 3 million people lived in England. There are over 50 million today. There were three sheep to every person!

The houses in a typical village would have been rebuilt many times since it was founded.

But each time they were built of simple materials such as mud and thatch that do not stand the test of time. The buildings would not be in orderly rows, but lay scattered about, each with a kitchen garden growing food for the family.

All village houses had space outside for a kitchen garden, **midden** (muck heap) and for jobs such as brewing and **tanning**.

Did you know... ?

- In Tudor times, most of England was still forested. People still used rivers to get from place to place wherever they could.
- During Tudor times, the wealthy moved out of their castles and built new stately homes.
- At the start of Tudor times the Roman Catholic church in England was very wealthy because it owned so much land.

Here is the view from the lord's castle looking over the church and a scattering of houses that make up the village.

Q **Which buildings in this picture are made from stone?**

Village life

In early Tudor times most people worked long hours and had little money. But as more people became wealthier, markets were held every week or even every day.

A Tudor market was more like a 'car boot sale'. Market stalls were set up to sell all kinds of things, both good and bad, old and new. You could buy a pig, bread, beer, salted meat, leather, lace, clothes, knives and even spices.

The market square was the heart of the village. It was also the place where wrongdoers were punished in the public pillory.

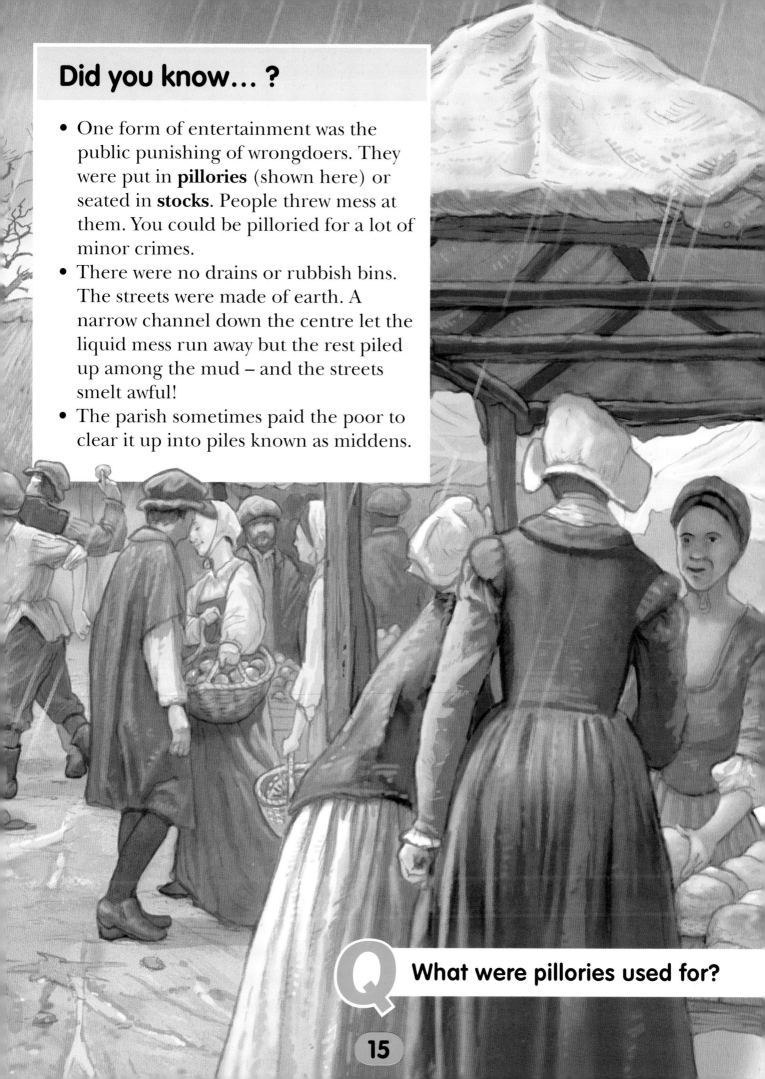

Did you know… ?

- One form of entertainment was the public punishing of wrongdoers. They were put in **pillories** (shown here) or seated in **stocks**. People threw mess at them. You could be pilloried for a lot of minor crimes.
- There were no drains or rubbish bins. The streets were made of earth. A narrow channel down the centre let the liquid mess run away but the rest piled up among the mud – and the streets smelt awful!
- The parish sometimes paid the poor to clear it up into piles known as middens.

Q What were pillories used for?

Tudor town

Towns were not planned and grew into a tangle of buildings. But the main street was lined with inns, the warehouses of merchants and the workshops of craftsmen. People made wagons and barrels, forged **scythes** and knives, carved chairs and stools and sold cloth and clothes.

The wealthier trades were in the middle of the town, while the smellier, poorer and more dangerous trades, such as tanners and brickmakers, were forced to be on the edge.

Towns had many craftsmen. Some had important buildings like abbeys.

Did you know... ?

- Most people in a town lived and worked in the same room.
- If you were a wealthy merchant, a squire or a lawyer, or even a very skilled craftsman, you could afford to have a bigger house with two or three storeys.
- Tanners were always on the edge of town. Tanning hides to make leather was a hot, smelly job – tanning was done in big vats of boiling urine! The waste also drained into rivers. No wonder no one drank river water!

Q Why did tanners live on the edge of town?

An Elizabethan town street

By Elizabethan times towns were getting crowded as people left farm land and looked for other jobs that paid more money.

One way to get more people into a house was to add upper floors. Another way was to build on what had once been back gardens.

These shabbily-built and small houses, were where poor families rented one room each.

The houses were mostly made of wood. They were built so close together that there was a great risk of fire spreading through the town. Few people had toilets, so the town was also very smelly.

The main street in an Elizabethan town.

Did you know... ?

- Towns could not spread out like they do today because nearly everyone had to get about on foot.
- That the roads were simply earth.
- That merchants and craftsmen advertised their business with signboards that hung outside their shops. They did not use writing because so few people could read.
- Signboards often fell down and hurt passers by.

Q **Why were the buildings so close together?**

Better times for some

In Tudor times the people who had more money made many changes to their homes. Extra rooms and floors were added, and some were completely rebuilt of better materials.

The most important change was to add a chimney using the newly invented bricks. This gave space for many other improvements as you will see in this picture.

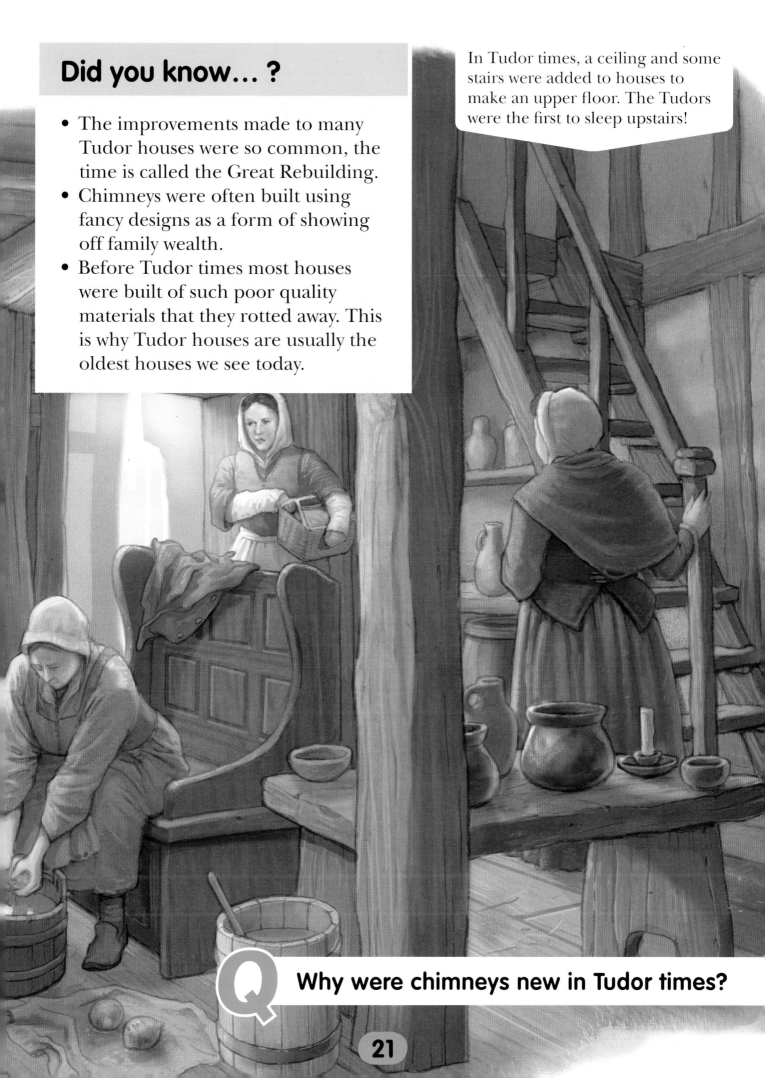

Did you know... ?

- The improvements made to many Tudor houses were so common, the time is called the Great Rebuilding.
- Chimneys were often built using fancy designs as a form of showing off family wealth.
- Before Tudor times most houses were built of such poor quality materials that they rotted away. This is why Tudor houses are usually the oldest houses we see today.

In Tudor times, a ceiling and some stairs were added to houses to make an upper floor. The Tudors were the first to sleep upstairs!

Q **Why were chimneys new in Tudor times?**

21

Rooms to let

Most poor families rented one room in a slum house in a side alley.

Their room had no water and no toilet. The upper rooms may not even have had a grate for a fire. It was cramped, cold, damp and dirty – a recipe for disease and early death.

This house was designed to be rented out. It is poorly made and the rooms are small.

Did you know… ?

- People used a bucket as a toilet. The contents of the buckets were poured out of the window and into the street.
- Toilet paper had not been invented in Tudor times.
- The upper storeys jutted out, giving more space to upper rooms. This is called jetting.
- Rats often infested the slums and disease was common. When someone got a disease called **plague**, a red cross was painted on the door as a warning to keep away.

Q **Why did people pour their waste out of upstairs windows?**

23

What Tudor wills tell us

We know so much about what many Tudor people owned and what they did because they wrote very detailed **wills**.

We can see what was important to people by looking at wills at the start and end of Tudor times. For example, as people became wealthier they bought what they called 'joined-up furniture', and from which we get the word joinery. It was harder to make and so cost more. You had to be better off to afford it.

At the start of Tudor times, people had few possessions and worried more about (Roman Catholic) priests saying prayers for them after they died. So they left money for this purpose. For example, this is the will of a reasonably well off (yeoman) farmer.

JOHN DOE, died 1 June 1492. To be buried in the churchyard of St. James. Payment of prayers: To the light of the Holy Cross 20d., of Blessed Mary the Virgin 16d., St. James 12d., St. Nicholas 12d., St. Christofer 16d., Blessed Mary of Pitee 16d. The lights of St. Blasé and St. Michael 12d. To repair of the church bells 20s.

My wife shall give to Willy, my son, when he comes of age of 22, 30 sheep, 4 oxen and 3 horses. Anything left should go to my wife.

(s means shillings; d means pence in old money)

FRANK DOE died 1 June 1592. To my son, my house, my clothes, including a coat, a pair of trousers, a bonnet (hat), a cloak, doublet, sword and dagger, and a saddle. To my wife: two cooking pots, a plate, a pewter dish, a pair of candle-holders, a silver spoon, bowls, a tub for brewing beer, a barrel, a cutting board, a set of scales and weights, a bed 'joined', a feather mattress and pillow, two pairs of sheets, blankets, a desk, a table 'joined', a cupboard, a long wooden seat, a bench, a chair, a spinning wheel and a chest.

(Notice that when he died *all* the things in the house were, by law, his – not his wife's. If he wanted his wife to have anything, he had to say so in his will.)

In later Tudor times, many people were both Protestant and wealthier, so they had more goods to pass on. For example, this is the will of an ordinary craftsman, Frank Doe, a skinner (of animals).

As some people got wealthier, so they could afford a four-poster bed and a mattress. This is 'joined-up' furniture.

Planks and a simple mattress were common before late Tudor times.

 What did people use before joined-up furniture?

Learning

Tudors had to pay for schooling. The very rich paid for a private teacher to come to their home. He was called a tutor.

The reasonably well off sent their sons to private schools. (In Tudor times no-one thought of educating girls).

The less well off tried to get their sons training in a trade. This was called an apprenticeship. They still had to pay for this. The poorest got no education at all. This meant that most people could not read or write.

Did you know... ?

- Lessons were given in Mathematics, Greek and Latin only.
- Discipline was very strict and pupils were often whipped. Many schools had whipping posts in their yards.
- The teacher had a uniform.
- Many monks became teachers. They were educated people and they had no other way of earning a living after their monasteries were closed by Henry VIII.

Tudor children wrote with a quill pen (a goose feather with the end cut off at an angle) and ink on **parchment**.

The time to the end of the lesson was marked out by using an hourglass filled with sand *(left)*.

This drawing shows later Tudor times. You can tell that because the boys and the teacher have ruffs (see page 9)

Q **Why did many monks become teachers?**

What can we see of Tudor times?

Today there are still many villages and towns with some Tudor buildings in them. Most are timber (wood), but some are brick and some are of stone.

The timber ones are the easiest to spot. There is one in the picture below. It has small windows and oak beams on the outside. It's called a 'black and white', or 'magpie' house. The other buildings are made of brick and have bigger window panes. They were built after Tudor times.

Many Tudor buildings are small. The reason they are often squashed in between other buildings is that their original neighbours have fallen down from old age and poor materials or been knocked down by people who did not see the point in looking after them.

TUDOR HOUSE
Antiques and Collectables
HENLEY 573680

TUDOR HOUSE

Many stately homes built in Tudor times survive. This is the grandest of all – Hampton Court. It was made of brick (see chimneys) and then **faced** with stone.

Many of the best preserved Tudor buildings are in small country towns which have not changed much over the centuries.

Q **Where is your nearest Tudor building?**

Try these...

Make a pomander for sweetening the air

- Use an orange with a stalk and tie a piece of string to the stalk. The string is for hanging the pomander up.

- Stick some cloves through the orange skin.

- Place two teaspoonfuls of ground cinnamon in a bowl and roll the orange in it, pressing the powder into the skin.

- Wrap the orange in tissue paper and keep in a warm dark cupboard for 2–3 weeks.

- Take out the pomander and hang it up.

Make a plague mask

In Tudor times the sickness called the plague was a killer. Doctors wore a plague mask because they thought it would protect them. They wore a cloth over their heads and faces and a 'beak' to cover their noses. The beak had herbs in to cover up the smell of the sick people.

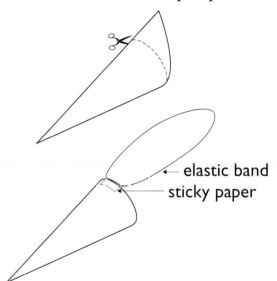

← elastic band
— sticky paper

- Fold a piece of A4 thin card to make a cone. Use sticky tape to fix it in place.

- Cut off the spare paper as shown.   .

- Make two holes at the side and thread a piece of elastic through them. Use enough to go over your head and hold the beak against your face.

- Place a piece of lavender or other herb in the beak and then put the beak on.

Make a family tree

The House of Tudor

Henry VII ═══╤═══ **Elizabeth**
1485–1509 │ *daughter of Edward IV*

A family tree shows related people using vertical and horizontal lines. Left is the Tudor tree started for you. Copy this out and complete the tree using the description below:

Henry VII and his wife Elizabeth had four children: Arthur (who died young), Henry, Mary and Margaret. Henry married 6 wives (find out their names on page 4). He had three children: Mary, Elizabeth and Edward. Margaret married James IV of Scotland and they had a son James. He married Marie and they had a daughter, Mary (Queen of Scots). Mary married Louis XII of France and then the Duke of Suffolk. They had a daughter Frances who married Henry Grey. Their daughter was Lady Jane Grey. Find out as a project, who Mary Queen of Scots and Lady Jane Grey were and why Queen Elizabeth did not like them.

Make a ruff

A ruff was worn around the neck by wealthy men and women in Elizabethan times.

- To make the ruff take a piece of A4 paper and cut it in half lengthwise.

- Fold one piece in half lengthwise and then cut it as shown below.

- Pull the ruff out slightly, then place it around your neck, pulling it out until it fits. Use a paperclip to fasten the ends.

FOLD

Glossary

civil war A war between peoples within the same country.

faced To add thin sheets of stone to the outside of a building for decoration only.

merchants People who trade in goods.

midden A dung heap or refuse heap.

parchment The skin of a sheep or goat prepared to make a material on which to write. It was very expensive.

pillory A wooden frame used for holding the hands and neck of wrongdoers while they were punished by having mess thown at them.

plague A serious and often fatal infection accidentally passed to humans by the bite of a flea that has bitten an infected rat.

ruff A stiffly starched frilled or pleated circular collar of lace, muslin, or other fine fabric, worn in Elizabethan times.

scythe A curved blade on a handle used for cutting crops.

spice A strongly smelling plant such as cinnamon or nutmeg.

stately home A very large house built on a grand scale, belonging to wealthy and powerful people.

stocks Frames for hands and feet in which the wrongdoer sat to be punished.

tanning Making leather from raw hides skinned from animals.

Tudors Kings and queens who reigned between 1485 and 1603.

will A legal document stating a person's wishes regarding what should happen to their property when they die.

Index

Curriculum Visions

Curriculum Visions Explorers
This series provides straightforward introductions to key worlds and ideas.

You might also be interested in
Our slightly more detailed book, 'Rich and poor in Tudor times'. There is a Teacher's Guide to match 'Rich and poor in Tudor times'. Additional notes in PDF format are also available from the publisher to support 'Exploring Tudor times'. All of these products are suitable for KS2.

Dedicated Web Site
Watch movies, see many more pictures and read much more in detail about the Tudors at:

www.curriculumvisions.com
(Professional Zone: subscription required)

A CVP Book
Copyright © 2007 Earthscape

First reprint 2008

Author
Brian Knapp, BSc, PhD
Educational Consultants
JM Smith (former Deputy Head of Wellfield School, Burnley, Lancashire); the Librarians of Hertfordshire School Library Service
Senior Designer
Adele Humphries, BA
Editor
Gillian Gatehouse
Photographs
The Earthscape Picture Library, except *The Granger Collection, New York* p4, 5.
Illustrations
Mark Stacey, except p4–5 David Woodroffe
Designed and produced by
Earthscape
Printed in China by
WKT Company Ltd

Exploring Tudor times
– *Curriculum Visions*
A CIP record for this book is available from the British Library

ISBN 978 1 86214 205 3

This product is manufactured from sustainable managed forests. For every tree cut down at least one more is planted.